Stone Age Bone Age!

Mick Manning · Brita Granström

W

FRANKLIN WATTS

NEW YORK·LONDON·SYDNEY

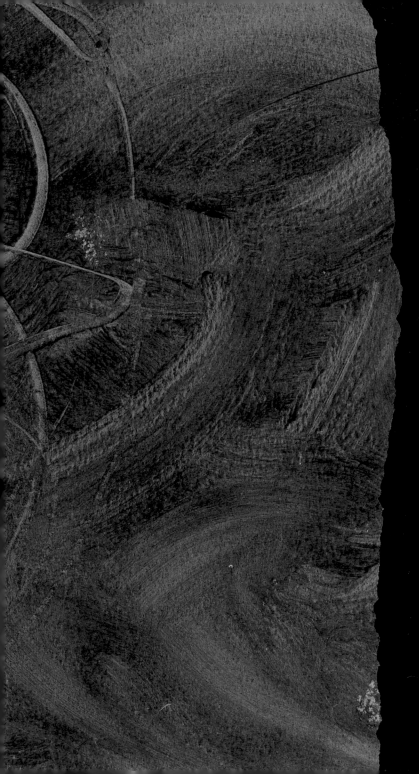

Listen – water dripping!
Wind moaning!
You've woken up in a dark cave.
You've woken up in the stone age!
No light switch, no window.
Feel your way towards the sound
of voices . . .

This story happens 12,000 years ago
when people used stone, bone, wood
and animal skin to make everything.

Outside there's a stone age family.
Mums, dads, grans, grandads . . .
aunties, uncles, cousins . . .
All getting ready to go hunting,
all getting ready to gather
wild food!

People lived in large family groups back then. It was safer that way, and easier to find food.

4

5

You go too! Let them show you
where to gather seeds and berries,
where to find the best honey,
where to dig for beetle grubs . . .

bird's egg

There were no shops in those
days! People hadn't even found
out how to grow things.

nuts

berries

Food had to be hunted and
gathered from the wild.

7

You go too!
Hunt the lake for fish
and water birds.
Learn how to paddle
a dug-out canoe . . .

A dug-out canoe was a log
hollowed out with fire
and stone tools.

Stone age people probably also
used skin canoes, coracles
and rafts.

9

Or try to tickle trout
in fast-flowing streams.
Flip them on the bank
with just a flick of your wrist!

Salmon and trout were either 'tickled'
or harpooned as they gathered to
lay their eggs.

male salmon

harpoon

Sun-dried fish would keep all winter!

Make tricky traps and track wild animals.

Hunting and trapping animals may seem cruel now, but it was a matter of survival then...

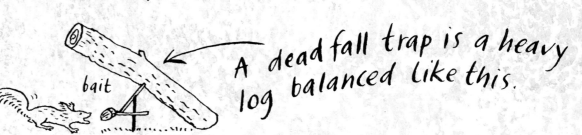

bait

A dead fall trap is a heavy log balanced like this.

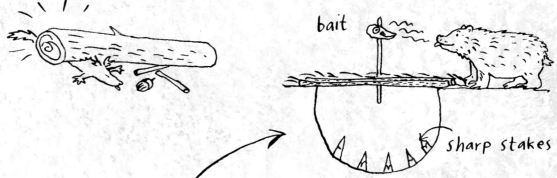

bait

sharp stakes

A pitfall trap is a hole in the ground covered with sticks and grass.

But be careful!
They may be tracking you. . .

Hunters used a spearthrower like this. . .

It gave a lot more power to the spear so it went much further.

15

What's this?
An ambush . . . Shhh!
A herd of woolly mammoths?
And they're getting closer . . . Shhh!
Now! Jump up and chase them . . .
Stone age, bone age!
Food for a month!

Just one mammoth would feed a
stone age family for weeks!
Nothing was wasted: meat and
fat were eaten, the skin was
used for keeping warm, tusks
and bones were used for tools,
carvings or fuel for the fire.

Would you treasure
a necklace of animals' teeth –
or a pendant shaped
like a flying bird?

Stone age, bone age.
You're one of the family now . . .

Stone age people felt happy and sad just like we do.

Many birds fly away in winter and come back in the spring. The bird pendant may have reminded people that life always begins again.

Back at camp, learn the art of knapping flint, or skinning a deer. Learn how to carve bone and antler. You can even make skin clothes!

Hardly anyone can do these things today- but just about everyone knew how to do them then...

flint spear point

Flint was the most useful stone, it could be chipped into sharp knives and spears.

A spear thrower beautifully carved from antler.

21

The Sun's going down. Quick, light a fire!
It keeps wild beasts away!
Quick, light a fire! It cooks our food.
Eat with your fingers –
it's a stone age barbecue!

There were no matches in those days – fire was made by rubbing sticks together or striking a spark with a flint.

Animal bones and other food remains like nut shells are sometimes found where prehistoric people lived.

Now it's time to visit
the magic place.
Deep in the cave,
by smoky torch-light,
the walls come alive!

Heartbeat . . .
Drumbeat . . .

Prehistoric cave art has been found all over the world. Perhaps people thought their paintings gave them magic powers over the animals they hunted.

Stamp like a stag!
Strut like a bird!
Growl like a bear!

Stone age! Bone age!
Howl like a wolf!

Stone age! Bone age!
What a clever age!

Stone Age! Bone Age! What a clever age!

Tracking wild animals

Making traps

Gathering nuts and berries

Tickling trout

Drying fish

Coming back to camp

28

Hunting mammoths

Spearing fish and waterbirds

Canoeing

Carving tusks, bones and antlers

Making tools

knapping flints

Scraping skins

Making skin clothes

29

Stone Age! Bone Age!

The stone age describes a time when people used stone to make their tools, before they learnt how to use metals like bronze and iron. The stone age is divided into many different periods. Our family live in a period we call the Upper Palaeolithic, about 12,000 years ago.

It is difficult to say when the stone age began and ended. The very first people used stone tools over two million years ago and a few people began to make metal tools about 7,000 years ago. The stone age did not end suddenly but slowly, over thousands of years, as more and more people learnt how to use metal. In some far away places, people still use stone tools today.

Helpful Words

Antlers – The 'horns' on a deer. Ancient peoples shaped the tough, bone-like antlers into tools. See page 21.

Beetle grubs – Beetles are grubs when they first hatch out from the egg. They live in dead wood and under the soil. See page 6.

Cave paintings – Pictures painted by people on the walls of caves thousands of years ago. They often painted pictures of the animals they hunted. See page 25.

Coracle – A coracle is a boat made of skins stretched around a wicker or wooden frame. See page 9.

Dogs – The first dogs were tame wolves. Over time, people changed the shapes and sizes of dogs by breeding them to help with different jobs, such as hunting or guarding.

Flint – A stone used by stone age people to make tools and weapons. See pages 21, 22.

Knapping – The way flint is chipped to make sharp cutting edges. See page 21.

Mammoth – A large, hairy elephant-like animal that is now extinct. There were various different types of mammoth. The woolly mammoth is shown in this book. It lived in cold regions of Europe, Asia and North America during the last ice age. See page 16.

Pendant – A pendant is a single piece of jewellery that people hang on something, such as leather thong, around their neck. See page 18.

Prehistoric – We say something is prehistoric if it comes from a time before people invented writing. See pages 22, 25.

Spear thrower – A tool used by stone age people that helped them throw a spear further and more accurately than they could by hand. See pages 15, 21.

Tracking – The skill of following animals by understanding the signs they leave behind, such as footprints and droppings. See pages 13, 15.

For all our ancestors . . .

First published in 2000 by Franklin Watts,
96 Leonard Street, London EC2A 4XD

Franklin Watts Australia
14 Mars Rd
Lane Cove
NSW 2066

Series editor: Rachel Cooke
Art director: Jonathan Hair
Consultant: Dr Alison Roberts, Ashmolean Museum, Oxford

Printed in Singapore
A CIP catalogue record is available from the British Library.
Dewey Classification 930.1
ISBN 0 7496 3536 3